A Dog's Life

First published by Parragon in 2009

Parragon
Queen Street House
4 Queen Street
Bath BA1 1HE, UK

Copyright © Parragon Books Ltd 2009
Design by Pink Creative Ltd

ISBN: 978-1-4075-8645-8

Printed in China

A Dog's Life

inspiration for dog lovers everywhere

PaRragon

Bath New York Singapore Hong Kong Cologne Delhi Melbourne

A dog is man's best friend.

Dogs are miracles

with paws.

Susan Ariel Rainbow Kennedy (Attrib), Author

A good dog deserves a good bone. Proverb

The reason a dog has

so many friends

is that he

wags his tail

instead of his tongue.

Unknown

There is
no psychiatrist in the world

like a

puppy

licking your face. Bern Williams, Author

The
biggest
dog

has been a

pup.

Joaquin Miller, Poet

15

A dog is one of the remaining reasons

why some people can be persuaded

to go for a walk.

OA Battista, Author

My little dog—a **heartbeat** at my feet.

Edith Wharton, Novelist

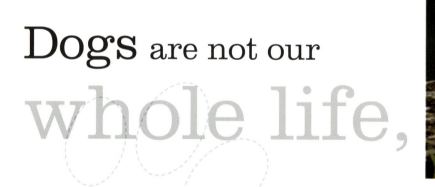

Dogs are not our whole life, but they make our

lives whole.

Roger Caras, Wildlife photographer

If your dog doesn't

like someone

you
probably
shouldn't
either.   Unknown

To live long,

eat like a cat,

drink

like a dog. German proverb

Dogs feel very **strongly** that they should always go with you in the car,

in case the need should arise for them to **bark** nothing

right in your ear.

Dave Barry, Columnist

A door

is what a dog is

perpetually on the

wrong side of.

Ogden Nash, Poet

If you can look
at a dog and not feel

vicarious
excitement

and affection,

you must be a cat.

Unknown

31

Anybody who doesn't know what soap

tastes like

has never

washed a dog.

Franklin P Jones, Businessman

The dog

was created specially for children.

He is the god of frolic.

Henry Ward Beecher, Minister

Yesterday I was a dog.
Today I'm a dog.
Tomorrow I'll probably

still be a dog.
Sigh!

There's so little hope for
advancement.

Charles M Schulz, Cartoonist

Don't accept

your dog's admiration

as conclusive evidence

that you are wonderful.

Ann Landers, Columnist

My goal in life is to be as good as my dog already thinks I am.

Unknown

a person

No matter how little money

having a dog makes

and how few possessions you own,

you rich.

Louis Sabin, Author

The cat will mew and the dog will have his day.

William Shakespeare, British poet and playwright

It is nought good

a sleeping

hound wake.

Geoffrey Chaucer, British author and poet

Dogs are better
than human beings
because they know
but do not tell.

49

A puppy is but a dog,

plus

high spirits,

and

minus

common sense.

Agnes Repplier, Essayist

Every dog is a lion at home.

HG Bohn, British publisher

Dachshund:

a half-a-dog high

and a

dog-and-a-half long.

Henry Louis Mencken, Journalist

The difference
between cats and dogs is,

dogs come

when they are called,

cats take a message

and get back to you.

Unknown

Man

is a dog's **idea**

of what God should be.

Holbrook Jackson, British journalist

There is no faith which has never been broken, except that of a truly

faithful dog.

One reason

a dog can be such a comfort

when you're feeling blue

is that he doesn't try

to find out why.

Unknown

Properly
trained,
a man can be
a dog's
best
friend.

Corey Ford, Humorist and author

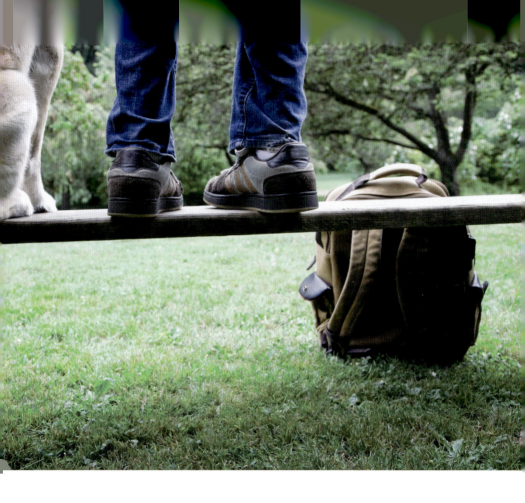

When a dog wants to hang out the

"Do Not Disturb"

sign, as all of us do now and then, he is regarded as a

traitor

to his species.

Ramona C Albert

The most **affectionate**
creature
in the **world**

is a wet dog.

Ambrose Bierce, Journalist

Life is like a dog sled team.

If you ain't the lead dog,

the scenery never changes.

Lewis Grizzard, Writer

If you stop every time a dog barks, your road will never end.

Saudi Arabian proverb

Women and cats will do as they please, and men and dogs should relax and get used to it.

Robert A. Heinlein, Novelist

No one appreciates
the very special genius
of your conversation
as the dog does.

Christopher Morley, Journalist

Did you ever **walk** into a room and forget why you walked in?

I think that is how dogs **spend** their lives.

Sue Murphy

A dog can **express** more with his **tail** in seconds than his **owner** can express with his **tongue** in hours.

Unknown

A dog
has the soul
of a philosopher.

Plato, Greek Philosopher

You can tell by the kindness of a dog how a human should be.

Don van Vliet, Musician

You can run
with the big dogs
or sit on the porch
and bark.

Unknown

A dog is the
only thing
on earth
that loves you
more than he loves
himself.

Josh Billings, Writer and humorist

A dog owns nothing,

yet is seldom

dissatisfied.

Irish proverb

I've seen a look in dogs' eyes, a quickly vanishing look of amazed contempt, and I am convinced that basically dogs think humans are nuts.

John Steinbeck, Writer

Every dog
has his day

but the nights
are reserved for the cats.

Unknown

Picture credits